T0381036

KNOTTY TREES

SHERRY RIGGS

Balboa Press books may be ordered through booksellers or by contacting:

Balboa Press
A Division of Hay House
1663 Liberty Drive
Bloomington, IN 47403
www.balboapress.com
844-682-1282

ISBN: 978-1-9822-6598-4 (sc)
978-1-9822-6600-4 (hc)
978-1-9822-6599-1 (e)

Library of Congress Control Number: 2021905953

Print information available on the last page.

Balboa Press rev. date: 04/26/2021

KNOTTY TREES

Photography and Poetry
by
Sherry Riggs

A MESSAGE TO MY READERS

Welcome to a journey.

A collection of
arboreal illusions.

See, what you see.

Imagine!

Knotty Trees.

Discover the artist
that resides in you.

Find yourself in a new view
of nature,
an artistic vision.

A gift
God gives us.

Enjoy your journey.

Blend yourself into the trees.

Love,
Sherry

TABLE OF CONTENTS

Expand your vision of the natural world
by looking through the eyes of artist Sherry Riggs.

Arboreal illusions were first inspired
during a walk on a twenty-acre wood
in Northern California.

I looked into the sunlight
glimmering through the limbs and leaves,
I noticed a tall, beautiful goddess torso,
lifelike, sleek, powerful, alive.

I couldn't get enough of her.

At that moment I felt a shift of what is possible,
a God-given gift with this new vision I just discovered.

My journey began.

A new adventure into the
purpose for my life.

A new view, exciting, fun, adventurous, creative.

Igniting the artist within myself and others.

Standing in the future,
enjoy the journey with me.

I share with you what I see.

Share with me what you see.

KNOTTY TREES

Standing In The Future
as far as I could see.

Mountains and hillsides,
to the east,
west to the sea.

Little did I know
that the existence
of my beautiful torso
would be the beginning
of a world I didn't know.

Who would have seen
the beauty in me,
the beginning of
a new possibility?

This new view
has transformed the fantasy,
into reality.

Let me introduce you to
TheArtistTree.

Standing In The Future

In the beginning,
would you believe,
the creation of
Adam and Eve.

I'm knot an apple tree.

Adam and Eve

Man came along
for all to see.

He was knot only
a primitive man,
he's also a KNOTTY TREE.

Climb on me.

Be free.

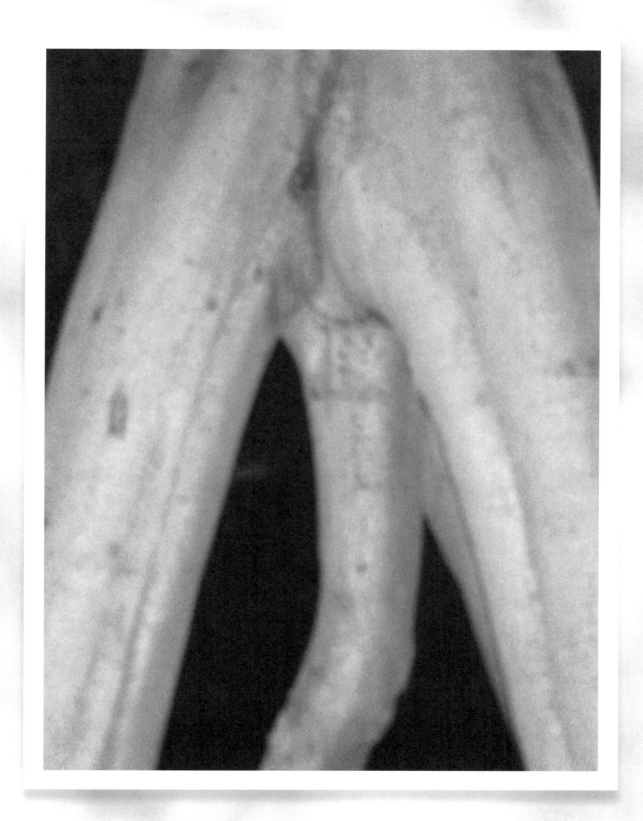

Man

Strolling along
and what do I see?

A beautiful woman
in the shape of a tree.

Purity, beauty, virginity.

Grounded in the earth,
her roots beneath me.

What do you see
in this tree?

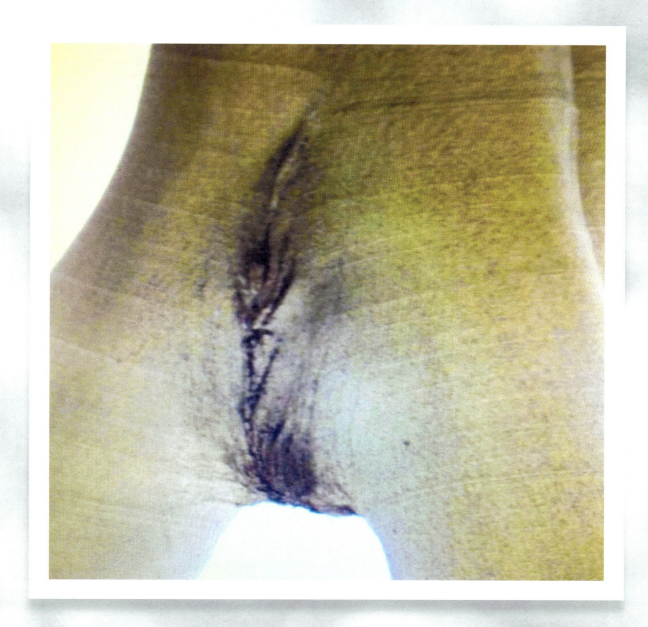

Woman

Mother Nature,
Autumn is here.

Shedding the past,
at last.

A new skin,
begin,
again.

Creation!

Be free,
being a
KNOTTY TREE.

Mother Nature

Don't be surprise
when you see me.

Remember,
I am a
KNOTTY TREE.

Rooted to the earth,
connected to the sea.

I am Sire,
king of all trees.

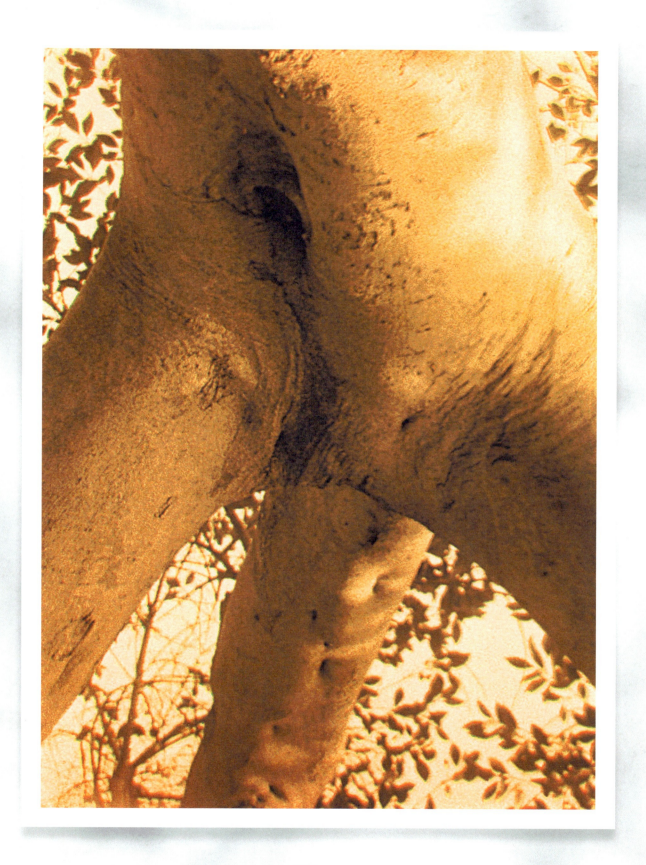

Sire

It's knot hard to see the breast,
that rests on the side of this tree.

What you can't see,
is her body.

Is she human, or knot?

A beautiful Female,
that's what I got.

What do you think
is connected
to this
KNOTTY TREE?

Female

Don't stop.

You're almost to the top.

Climb the tree
that lives by the sea.

Climb one branch at a time,
to see the horizon
at the end of the sea.

What awaits at the top
is knot a fantasy.

The sunset.
Ecstasy!!

The Climb

Your branches, are your wings,
growing towards the sunlight,
reaching for the sky
'til the sun sets into the night.

Nocturnal creatures rest and nest,
from your branches take flight,
freedom to be,
what God meant them to be.

Awakening.

Your beauty breathtaking,
God pulling you to the sky.

Spread out your branches,
your wings in the breeze.

Fly.

Be free.

Angel of Beauty Tree.

Angel of Beauty

Beautiful me,
tall, slim, innocent, tree.

Fertile seeds rooting beneath me,
reaching for the future
designed for me.

Pollen dancing in nature's breeze,
resting on my branches and leaves.

The breeze divine
in harmony with the sea,
springtime ecstasy.

Good-bye Innocence.

My destiny.

Innocence

Bliss,
sharing
The Kiss,
nature
making love
unnoticed,
'til I came along.
"Join us in our Bliss."
Now we are three,
you are a branch
of our KNOTTY TREE.

The Kiss

Sisters,
growing up together,
rooted in time.

I'm just seven years old,
you would be nine.

Protect me, big sister,
your shade
will make dew.

We'll always be growing,
into a new view.

Sisters

Little Brother,
you're growing up alone
hiding by the sea.

Trust me.

I will not
chop off your branches
that make you strong.

Stand tall, after all,
nothing is wrong.

Be proud of being a
KNOTTY TREE.

Little Brother

Imagine,
if you can,
a tree named Tarzan.

Who would think,
it's plain to see,
branches covering his privacy.

What's the chance
you could see,
Tarzan
being a tree?

Tarzan

Dance, Prance, Dance.

Swaying your branches
into night.

Sending the night owl
into flight.

Let go of your disability
you beautiful tree.

When morning comes,
birds will sing,
you will dance
to their melody.

Dance La Coca, Dance!

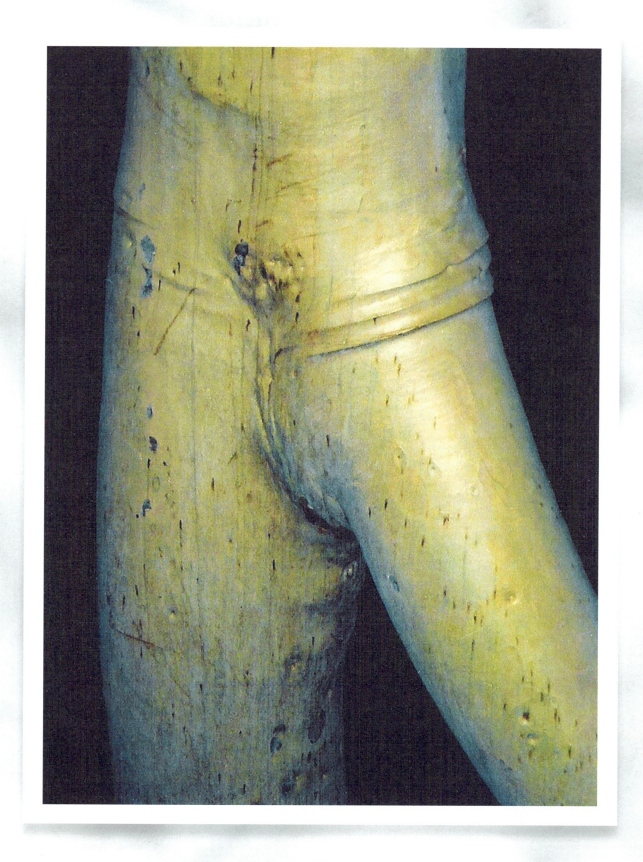

La Coca

Look once, look twice,
take a peek,
see what you see.

It could be two feet,
or maybe it's three.

A very large branch,
looks like a woody.

KNOTTY TREE!!

Woody

Don't be stubborn,
it's a tall price to pay,
your branches cut off that day.

No branching out into the future,
if not willing to grow.

Sway your
Stubby branch,
take a chance,
reach in the direction
you want to grow.

We don't know
what we don't know.

The possibility being a

KNOTTY TREE.

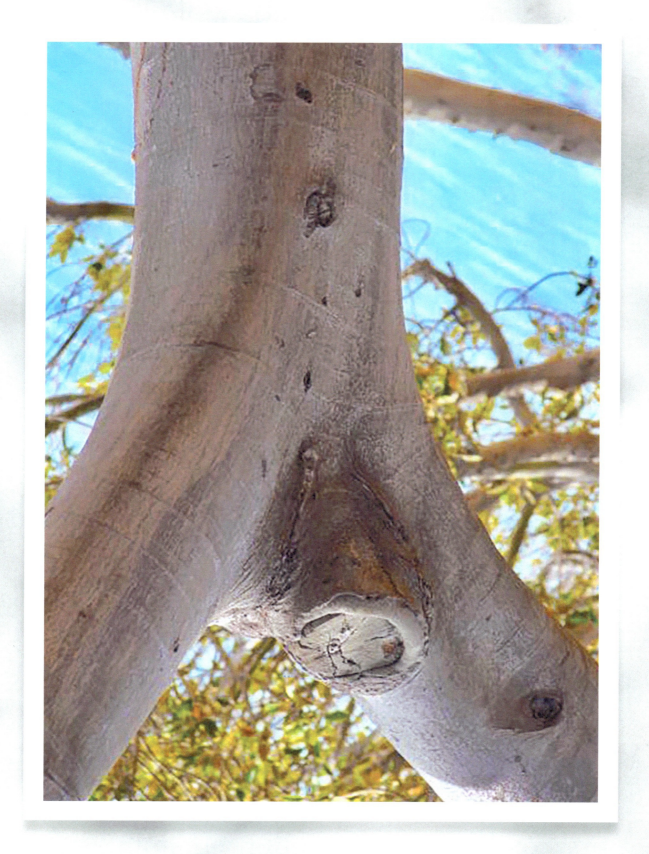

Stubby

Eve,
nude in the garden,
poised like a tree,
then came along,
TheArtistTree.

Surprised
to see her beauty,
her vanity,
free in the garden
amongst

KNOTTY TREES.

Eve

You're Exposed.

You can knot hide.

Your shield
has turned with the seasons
and does knot protect you anymore.

I see you.

Do knot pretend
to knot see me.

You
KNOTTY TREE.

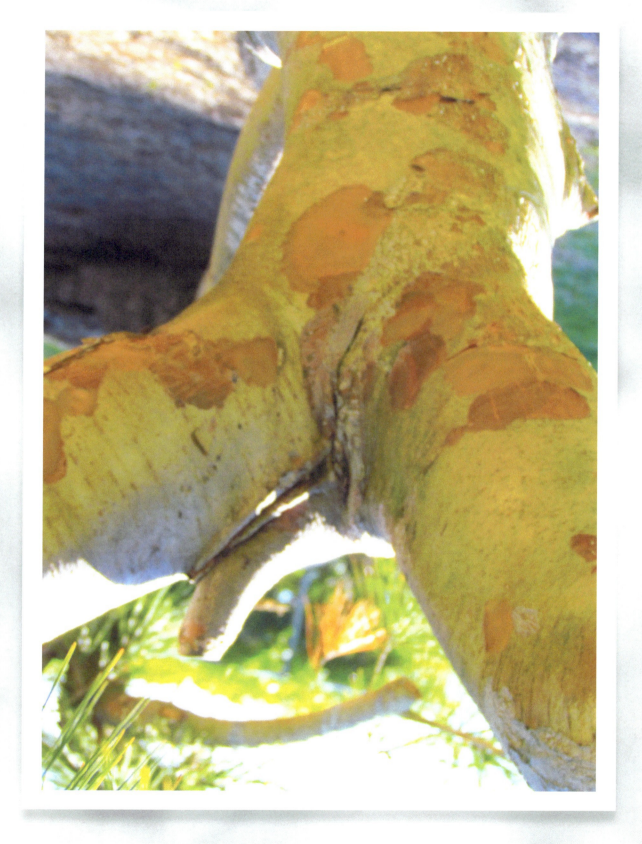

Exposed

Camouflaged, disguised,
how wise.

Hidden in the branches,
taking chances.

Surviving, unnoticed,
blending into nature's pallet.

Sire on the loose,
blowing pollen to the roots
of

The Huntress.

The Huntress

Walking on the path
by the Pacific sea.

Enjoying our earth
when I came upon this tree.

Head buried in the ground,
hiding, upside down.

Looking for her truth
Down Under.

Down Under

Resting quietly in the sunshine,
nature's palette blended,
so divine.

Ocean air spreading leaves,
sun rays beaming through the trees.

Her bark shedding,
composting the ground,
Vulnerable,
hoping never to be found.

Then SHE came along,
discovered me,
now, I'm a
KNOTTY TREE.

Vulnerable

Set me free
from Bondage,
roots
that bind me.

Set me free
into the sea.

Driftwood
once a tree,
floating
sea to sea,
fulfilling
her destiny.

Bondage

Dedicated to Victims
and Survivors of Breast Cancer.

Coming out of the cemetery,
carrying a sad heart,
I saw Prevention,
from the very start.

The spirit lead me
to this ribbon tree,
I knew in an instant
my friend was set free.

Heavenly.

Prevention

Mirror, mirror

on the wall,

here I stand

twenty-feet tall.

It's my body

that I see,

tree shaped as

GOD created me.

Reflection, Reflection

set me free,

behold,

a

KNOTTY TREE.

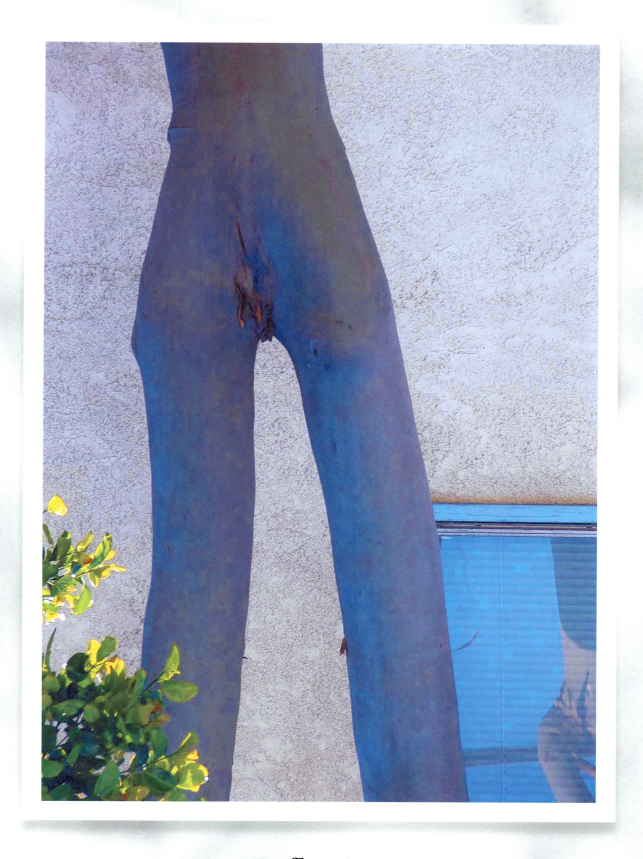

Reflection

ACKNOWLEDGEMENTS

Thank you, GOD, for my vision,
and for the artist in me.
We can look and sometimes don't see,
our beautiful planet, mountains, and seas.
Thank you, for our beautiful trees.

Thank you, my family, you're always there for me.
Play with your new vision, see what I see.
Now, it's part of our family tree.

Thank you, my lifetime clients, and friends,
my gratefulness to you never ends.
We go back, year after year,
sharing secrets, laughter, and tears.
Cheering me towards what I see,
you've always been part of my destiny.

Thank you, Bob Minor,
for all the hours you spent being my tutor,
overcoming the fear of my computer.
With all the laughter and fun,
and too Molly for cheering us on,
with love, and beyond.

Thank you, Robert Freeman,
for your counsel and seeing my vision for
KNOTTY TREES.

Thank you, Robert Beers,
for your time and expertise,
and setting it up in ID.

Thank you, authors,
Dr. Marjorie Miles, Lillian Nader,
Haley K.Wilson and Paula Blackwell.
You are the women that pulled out the poet
that resides in me.
You are the force behind me.

A special thanks to Beverly.
You are heavenly.
You know who you are for me.

Knotty Trees

Photography and Poetry
by
Sherry Riggs

Printed in the United States
by Baker & Taylor Publisher Services